Choices

Frank Chevannes

Dedication

This book is dedicated to my Grandmother.
Emeline Carol Chevannes

Forever in our hearts and minds

CONTENTS

Introduction

INTRODUCTION

I'm Frank Chevannes, a young black man raised in the UK, born in the Bahamas and of Jamaican descent.

I see life as a series of experiences. Some are highs and some are lows. How we choose to receive these experiences and what we decide to take from them impacts or shapes our future.

In this book, I'm opening up. I'll share the experiences that shaped me for one reason – to help you see that we always have the power of choice. My goal is to empower you to make the right choices to become the best version of yourself.

Most of my career has revolved around sales. This has enabled me to control my destiny and leverage my dominant strengths (such as drive, determination, competitiveness and a hunger for knowledge). I've also figured out how to compartmentalise my time and use what I've earned to create multiple streams of income which, in time, will allow me to shape the life of my dreams. Personality wise, I'm very driven; once I've set my sights on a goal, it's full steam ahead. Fortunately for me, I believe in myself and don't need anyone else to get me going. However, I am always there to help others who believe in themselves too. Sometimes all you need is a vote of confidence, nudge in the right direction or reminder that yes, you too can choose to design the life you have always dreamed of.

Let's begin.

1 CHOICE, INSTINCT, AND INTUITION

W hat is a choice? And how do we go about identifying the right choice when it presents itself?

According to the Oxford English dictionary, choice is defined as "an act of choosing between two or more possibilities; something that you can choose."

Not every choice we're presented with is truly a choice. It sounds funny, but it's true. Just look at politics – we're often forced to choose between the "lesser of two evils." Or think about those times you butt heads with those "my way or the highway" types. Spotting deception will pay dividends and protect you from moments of entrapment or coercion.

Let's briefly look at how we can use our instincts to our advantage and the roles our senses play in making choices.

Intuition is a sense that, if well-tuned, can play a major role in good decision-making. For the most part, intuition is subconscious but evidently present. For example, have you ever heard someone say, "I've got a bad feeling about this," or "something smells fishy," or "something doesn't look quite right?" Or, in contrast, "I've got a good feeling about this," or "sounds like a good idea," or "looks too good to be true." This is our subconscious mind drawing on experiences in our past and telling us to do or choose one thing over another. A familiarity exists that's been internally validated and makes perfect sense.

Emotions also impact our judgement too. We can all relate to a time in which we let emotions get the better of us. We certainly know it's easy to act on emotion rather than logic. Emotions can cloud our judgement and work against us – that's especially true if we're unaware of their presence and only realise their impact in hindsight. Always "think before you speak and act," – that's biblical advice, and it's useful in practice. Emotions, if left to run wild, can lead to a slew of terrible choices.

Here are two scenarios to break this down for you.

First scenario. I ask you to lend me £50 and from memory, everyone you've ever lent money to, always had an excuse when it came time to pay you back. Instantly, your "gut feeling" along with some protective or defensive anger and aggression, is going to tell you "don't do it!" That's a logical response.

Second scenario. I present you with an opportunity to invest a small amount of money, say £50, in a project I passionately articulated to you. The excitement may urge you to quickly reach for your phone to make the transfer.

Now in reality, nothing fundamentally changed between the two scenarios. I always needed £50 for something, but the words I used brought out different emotions from you and resulted in different outcomes. I'll explore the conscious and unconscious mind more in the next chapter.

The illusion of choice. This right here is how many people take advantage of and control others. Without diving too deeply into conspiracy theories, let's look at traditional schools and the prison system. Throughout school, we are told when to take a break, when to eat lunch, what topics or subjects we'll spend the most time on, where to sit in class, to only speak when spoken to after raising our hand and the list goes on. What kind of life is this really preparing us for? I've seen the school system compared to prisons and the similarities are striking. Dress code, emphasis on silence, walking in lines, lack of autonomy, minimal freedom and set times for pretty much everything. Erving Goffman, a Canadian social psychologist, refers to both as "total institutions." Yet, many of us believe that childhood provides us with the most freedom we'll experience before we hit the responsibilities of adulthood.

I, on the other hand, think the complete opposite. I believe as an adult, you truly have the freedom to choose your path as long as you have a growth mindset, which means being open to change, new ideas and adapting when necessary and adopt an "it's never too late to start" type of attitude.

Levi Roots, for example, brought us Reggae Reggae Sauce, a spicy sauce loaded with flavor, at 45 years old. He had been dubbed the "Dragon Slayer," successfully pitching on Dragons' Den and gaining investment backing from Peter Jones and Richard Farleigh. Within seven years, he built a net worth of £35m doing what he loved. That, for me, is freedom. You can watch this moment for yourself – search YouTube for "the most successful pitch in Dragons' Den history." Dragons Dens' YouTube channel has the video with that title. It wasn't a perfect pitch; there were a few hiccups. But Levi's choice to remain calm, confident and believe in himself made all the difference.

After finishing school in England, it's all on you; society has done its part and given you a "fair shake" in the system. Now, it's down to you to make it on your own. I would actually go as far as to say that from 16 years of age, you begin making the most important choices that will ultimately shape your future. Do you go to work, or do you further your education? Do you start a relationship, or do you spend time discovering yourself? Do you travel and explore or stick around where you grew up? Honestly, there are no true right or wrong answers here. What's more important is understanding that by making these seemingly simple choices, you're also impacting the direction of your life.

One of my favourite trilogy films is *The Matrix*. In the second film, *The Matrix Reloaded*, we're introduced to a character called the Merovingian, a villain who holds people captive and is keen to demonstrate his power and control over others. He tells Neo and Morpheus (the heroes in this film), that "choice is an illusion created between those with power and those without," and that "our only hope is to understand it, to understand the why." He goes on to show how he can effortlessly manipulate, among other things, a woman's emotions. What I believe they were trying to question here is, why are we here? And what is it we are supposed to do? It's a heavy conundrum when you stop and think about it.

And with that in mind, rather than settling for the status quo, I've decided to challenge this. I look at life as a movie because, come to think of it, **life is a movie. And when you realise you're in the movie, YOU'RE THE HERO OF YOUR OWN MOVIE.** Now, I don't think I'm bulletproof, and I can't fly, even though I wish I could. If anyone ever tells you to remember that you're "not the center of the universe," they're right – you're not. But don't let that change your perspective on your life because your world does revolve around you and the choices you make do shape it.

I empower myself to achieve whatever it is I choose to put my mind to. I found that goal setting works best for me – it is the tool I use to accomplish progress. It can do the same for you. Choose something you desire, whether personal or professional, make it specific, write it down, and put a time limit on it. Them, think of every step you need to take to get from where you are now to where you would like to be. This may mean sacrifice and lifestyle changes, but these critical choices will be the foundation upon which you'll build your success.

Pro-tip: set a high bar; pick goals that are out of your reach and out of your comfort zone. You'll be surprised by what you can achieve when you focus and put the effort in. It sounds cheesy, but it's true that "if you shoot for the moon, even if you miss, you'll land amongst the stars" - Norman Vincent Peale. I'll cover lifestyle more later.

Self-educate and develop as much as physically possible. **Education is one of the most powerful tools at your disposal,** but you have to choose to color outside the lines of the curriculum to give yourself a rounded view of the world.

2 LIFESTYLE, BLUEPRINTS AND GOLDEN TICKETS

How we spend our time outside of work shapes our views, beliefs and even our appearance.

I've already shared that I'm an aspirational character who always wants more. I'll be honest; I want the world and everything in it. I don't mean that literally. But if there is something I want to try or somewhere I'd like to go, I'll do everything in my power to make it a reality.

It's no good setting a huge goal if you lack the commitment and conviction to follow through. Many successful people throughout history have advised us to surround ourselves with people who bring out the best in us, want the best for us and will support us in chasing our dreams.

If you can also find people on the same wavelength chasing similar dreams, that's a bonus. You can take it a step further by adding people to your circle who have already achieved these goals. Then you'll be unstoppable. A blueprint to success is like a golden ticket; all you have to do is "just do it!" Nike put it best and that's the easiest choice you'll ever make if you ask me.

Over the years, my circle of friends has both grown and shrunk. The people in my circle have also changed. At this point, I have a few true friends that I can count on one hand and many associates. I'm okay with that. In fact, I prefer it.

Now I don't agree with Drake's "no new friends" lyric and mindset. I view that as ignorant and narrow-minded. You can never stop learning or growing as a person and that means you should never stop exposing yourself to new people.

Instead, take in this quote from Sir Isaac Newton. "If I have seen further, it is by standing on the shoulders of giants." He said that back in the 1600s. It's 2020 – all you have to do is look and you'll find knowledge and guidance in abundance. But if you close yourself off and decide that you already know it all, you're doing yourself a disservice.

After studying English, Media and Drama at A level or College, then Law at University there came a time when I was done with reading. I'd had enough, there wasn't anything I could do to motivate myself to pick up another book.

I knew this was hurting my mental growth, but I didn't see any way around it. Then I noticed I had a lot of time to spare while commuting to and from the office. I always chose to listen to music over reading and for a long time, I did nothing to change that.

I thought about getting a Kindle but never did. I even had an iPad for a good few years, but I never downloaded a single book to read on it. Instead, I filled it with music and movies. I couldn't shake how much I enjoyed the entertainment.

Luckily for me, something happened that set me on a new path and sped up my mental growth for good. The key? Audio books. Whoever invented them is a genius and I'm forever in their debt. Now, I can consume books in a few weeks with little effort. In the last six months, I've bought and listened to books from a range of diverse authors.

My favorites are:

When, by Daniel Pink. This book will give you tremendous insight into how you can use time to your advantage and uniquely understand for yourself when and why you perform at your best.

Natives, by Akala, will open your eyes and help you read between the lines in society. That's especially true if you fall into an ethnic minority group. Even if you don't, the book will show you the questionable choices made by The Empire – choices you did not learn about in school.

Switch, by Chip and Dan Heath, will guide you in creating change for the greater good in any scenario and teach you how to appeal to the emotional and rational mind. That's how you create lasting change.

Black Privilege, by Charlamagne Tha God, demonstrates the harsh reality that success is by no means a straight line, but if you stay true to yourself and "live your truth" the right people will see the value in your unique and authentic self

Finally, a book I've just finished, *Hustle Harder, Hustle Smarter* by none other than Curtis 50 Cent Jackson, will force you to shift gears and push forward.

If I truly gave up on reading, I would have never learned these lessons over the last year. Now, each month before I buy a movie or music, I'll buy an audiobook that can teach me something new. I've even got a few classic books like *The 48 Laws of Power* sitting in my audio library that I can't wait to break into. What can I say, I'm enjoying the growth?

All of the books I've just mentioned have taught me key lessons that I've chosen to implement in my own life and all, in turn, have led to personal growth.

Family. Time to get personal. At age 18, I chose to change my surname by deed poll and took my mother's maiden name. I felt that it was the right thing to do after my grandmother passed away. No one ever forced or asked me to do this – it was all by my own accord.

Recently, I was asked about my stance on women taking their husband's surname at marriage and if I agree or disagree with women who keep their family name and double barrel their surnames instead. I was also asked how I would feel if I was put in the position of giving my children that same double-barreled surname.

Over the years I've learned to avoid knee jerk reactions, as you may have gathered, this was a conversation I was having with a significant other.

I can't say that I'm against the idea because, as you've probably noticed by now, I'm no conformist. If I'm passionate about a particular topic, I have no problem going against the grain to change the status quo.

The way I see it, a mother and father's initial decision on a family name is irrelevant if there is no follow through. Bear with me here. I say it's irrelevant because I changed my surname at 18; my upbringing led me to make that choice.

My parents separated when I was still young. I saw my father from time to time, but if hard-pressed to share examples of fundamental moments in my childhood where I accomplished or achieved something substantial or learned about a new topic or even learned a new skill, every major influence came from someone on my mother's side of the family and believe me I've got endless examples there.

So, by the time I reached 18, I knew a lot about who I was on the inside and I also knew who I related to most in terms of family. So when my grandmother passed, it dawned on me that my family's namesake would eventually die too if I didn't do something to change it and that's a reality I'll have to accept. So, with all that passion inside, I chose to go against the grain and change my name.

My point is this – as a parent, if you don't choose to nurture your children, show them the value in having a family and provide what they need to grow into strong adults, at any point in the future, they may choose to undo your initial naming choice. So, the choice that is more important than the name is the choice to work hard at being a parent and show your children the value of family rather than forcing your family name on them. Give your children every reason to always want to choose your family name, that they'll carry on.

"You can choose your friends; you can't choose family" - Harper Lee. This great quote couldn't be truer and truthfully, I wouldn't change mine for the world as without them, I wouldn't have grown into the person I am today, sounds cliché but it's true. We are who we are, maybe that means some people get a bit of a head start on us in life, but life is a marathon and not a sprint to the finish. Take the good with the bad it builds balance and character; without the dark nights how can we ever appreciate the brighter days. My mother is like my backbone. You hear kids talk about their "day ones" – the ones they can always count on to be there for them when they need them the most. I know without a shadow of a doubt that if everyone I know turned their backs on me, if everything that I had fell apart and my world came crashing down, my mother would be there to catch me. That's just the person she is.

Being the youngest of three brothers, you could say I was born into competition. This is probably why competing to be the best comes naturally to me. As you can imagine, I lost a lot growing up, but I never gave up. I just saw it as growth and an opportunity to learn how to be better next time. I overcame the fear of losing at a young age. How do you compete with a brother who has two or five years on you? Who's taller than you, faster than you, and is able to hit harder than you can? it almost sounds impossible; impossible, that's my least favourite word in the English language. You win with patience. I'll admit I hate losing, but I'm not afraid of defeat. I expect competition in everything that I do.

Living a healthy lifestyle. If you ask anyone around me and I mean anyone, not just my friends, they will tell you "Frank knows the gym well." Yeah, I fall off sometimes, no one is perfect, but I always bounce back and keep myself in relatively good health.

Leading a healthy lifestyle keeps unhealthy weight off, gives you more energy, helps you think clearer, and even keeps you in a better mood more of the time.

The top two excuses I hear from most people if I engage them in this conversation is "I don't have the time" and "I hate running."

The time excuse is played out. Ask anyone to walk you through their day from start to finish and you'll soon spot the poor choices that lead to lack of time – too much time watching TV, sleeping, or lazing around on the sofa.

Now I understand the "I hate to run" point. I don't love it either. But I've learned the best thing to do is trick your brain by doing something else that burns the same number of calories you would've burned during a run.

This could mean taking up a solo or team sport, whichever works best for you or simply walking. During the lockdown, I've shared this a lot on social media – you can go for a walk for one hour a day and if you walk at a moderate pace, you'll burn a healthy 400 to 500 calories with little effort. Pick good routes that make for an interesting walk, so you don't get bored. Put together a playlist to keep you company if there's no one to walk with. Leading a healthy life seems like an obvious choice but every time I hear the statistics on the news it sounds like the majority of the nation would rather be unhealthy and overweight.

Exercising gives me a release and clears my mind. Nothing beats a heavy session in the gym after a tough day at the office.

Blow off steam. I've talked a lot about focus, drive, and goals. But in reality, you have to balance that out – you don't want to run yourself rampant. I don't mind going to a club, having a drink or just hanging out with friends. And I'll admit I can sometimes spend way too much time on social media; Instagram and YouTube can be addictive. So be sure to pursue balance. Without it, you'll drive yourself   crazy.

3 EDUCATION, CHOOSE TO COLOUR OUTSIDE THE LINES

Growing up, education was one of the most important things my mother made sure I had and valued. It came naturally to her being a teacher herself.

But when you look back at your years from 11 to 16, what did you learn from school? What did you gain? The two are very different. I learned most of what was put in the curriculum and benefited from being in one of the top sets, which means the top two classes for the year group. The lower down you go in terms of sets, the less chance you have of actually learning anything. Peer pressure drove those students to constantly act out, skip school, and generally be disruptive. This made it almost impossible for teachers to teach. I feel sorry for the kids in those classes who came to school and just wanted to do their best. I gained some core skills that I use daily, like English, Math (and occasional geography and history). If you ask me what I did not learn or gain, that list is longer. Personal finance, how to start a business, which political party best suits my viewpoint and how to protect myself from fraud, among others. To me, all of the above seem important for real life. But someone decided that memorising the periodic table was a higher priority. I wasn't fooled. I knew I needed to fill in the gaps.

Education comes in many forms, figure out what works best for you and double down. For example, growing up, I studied a range of martial arts from age 10 to 15. This included Tae Kwon Do, Wing Chun and Brazilian Jiu-Jitsu. Across all, I noticed a few constants. Discipline, resilience and perfection. Being sub-standards was not acceptable. How these values were instilled in me heavily out ways the methods used in traditional schools. Most of my teachers struggled to control the classroom, were unable to encourage resilience and they really had too much on their plate to demand the best from all of their students. Fortunately, for me, I did have a handful of teachers that you could say were one in a million – respected by their peers and students. I actually looked forward to their classes, it was always clear that they knew their topics inside and out. They were also well equipped to tackle the most challenging students.

Once you reach adulthood, you choose to either take the reins and elevate yourself or be left behind. So, ask yourself, what have you done lately to further your knowledge? Where have you looked? Who do you trust to provide you with the best information for you? I'm not expecting everyone to go back to school, college, or university and come out with degrees. The point I am making is taking a moment to look at your field of work or even your biggest passions.

Let's start with your field of work. Whatever stage you're at in your career, there is a way to get to the next stage faster. It will mean doing more than just showing up on time every day, doing your best work and hoping for a promotion. You'll need to ask questions that validate your work and performance and ask to be shown where you are and where you need to get to, to be ready and considered for the next level, Then, instead of just showing up, you can work towards this stage or level up and earn it. Choose to become a master within your field. Identify which of your skills and tools require the most work and make sacrifices to find time to do that internal work. What astounds me the most is that everyone knows when they need to bring their best and put in extra time in order to excel. This could be for a new job interview, a potential promotion or preparing for a big presentation. The choice to focus and change your attitude is what gets you to your best. Subconsciously, many of us regularly choose not to put in those extra hours or consistently perform at our best. I don't know why wanting to be the best version of yourself would be a part-time ambition. Imagine you paid a lot of money to get great seats to see an artist perform. Now imagine that the artist shows up and performs poorly, way less than you know their best to be, how disappointed you would be. Take that emotion and internalise it.

Using this same approach in pursuit of your passions can sometimes feel like walking a tightrope; if it becomes too serious, maybe it will no longer be fun. Personally, I've never had that thought or felt that way. I believe turning your passion into your career is a huge win and something to be proud of. If I'm interested in something, I'll seek out the knowledge of the best in the field, be it cooking, training, or photography. Take cooking, for example, YouTube has become my number one tool. To nail cooking a steak or roasting a leg of lamb, I can watch Gordon Ramsey do this step-by-step, performing at the highest standard. I practice until I get it just right, then I give myself creative license to adjust the recipe to my liking. But I'll become obsessed. I want to know all the finer details: what cut of lamb is Gordon using, are those dry herbs or fresh herbs, is he planning to roast on a tray or a rack? You can see my strive for perfection coming through. I love cooking and choose not to cook every day, but when I step into the kitchen to prepare a meal the anticipation for a tasty dish for friends and family excites me. I welcome that pressure. But I only arrived here by stepping out of my comfort zone, trying something new and learning from the best.

Education, unfortunately, isn't always this fun. Let's get serious for a second and talk about racism.

Racism is probably one of the poorest if not the, poorest choice ever made in history from one race to another, a choice that has plagued humanity for centuries. Being born in the Caribbean and being of Jamaican descent, it should come as no shock that I am a minority in one of the most powerful western countries, the United Kingdom. Being a minority, unfortunately, means and has always meant that I'm treated differently. Whether the actions that create these treatments are conscious or subconscious doesn't excuse them. In fact, the subconscious acts are worse, and they provide evidence of the horrible truth of systemic racism.

I won't cover old ground; you can pick up any book on civil rights, apartheid or segregation and gain a deep understanding of what my ancestors endured entering the western world. To briefly sum it up, my grandfather on my mother's side came to London in the Windrush. The Windrush generation, as they're known due the name of the ship's "Empire Windrush" which started transporting the mass migration from the commonwealth countries to Great Britain back in the 1940s following the end of the war. This didn't happen because Britain wanted to welcome in her distant countrymen with open arms. Instead, it happened because after the war, Britain needed labor and people with skills. Many women from the Caribbean came to work for the NHS, the National Health Service.

So, it's no surprise that shock broke out when, just a few years ago, the "Windrush Scandal" occurred. Members of the Windrush generation – many of whom were children when they came to Britain with their parents – received letters saying they had no right to be in the UK and that they were illegal immigrants who would lose their jobs, homes and would have no access to the NHS. it really is sickening. How can you be asked to come to Britain, as a British citizen, under the British Empire that colonized your homeland, work here for 60 years and then suddenly be told you're about to lose everything, it's disgraceful!

The other thing that baffles me is that year after year, institutions, global brands, and media rub racism in our faces simply because they can. In just the past few years, I've seen Serena Williams targeted by the Australian media and depicted in a cartoon as an ape-like figure. Google it and you'll see. After much investigation, they tell us it was ruled that this "did not breach media standards" so no punishment was dealt, or reform made. H&M, a brand I previously had no problems with, put out an ad with a young black boy wearing a jumper which read "coolest monkey in the jungle." Do you see a trend yet? The history of countless attempts to compare people of color to animals and dehumanizing them is overwhelming.

Let's look at another example. Former San Francisco 49ers quarterback Colin Kaepernick wanted to peacefully protest police brutality by kneeling during the national anthem before NFL games (previously, he would sit for the anthem, but a war veteran advised him that taking a knee would be more respectful). His industry, which had supposedly held him in high regard, turned its back on him. He has been unable to work in the NFL ever since.

You know the sounds of sirens and the sight of officers of the law in uniform has never comforted me. If anything, it's always made me feel threatened and uneasy. I can remember being 17 and on my way home from work. At the time, I worked part-time for Cecil Gee in Bluewater, one of the largest shopping malls in Kent. During my long bus ride home, there was an altercation on my bus evolving teenagers of different races surprise surprise. During this altercation, the police were called. They caught up with the bus, stopped it in its tracks, and came upstairs to investigate. The people involved were easily pointed out – just like after a boxing match, no one needs to ask who was fighting; it was blatantly obvious. Anyway, after the initial investigation, an officer approached me and asked if I was involved, where I was going, and said that he needed to search me. No one else on the bus received this treatment other than me, I wondered what was different about me, I didn't really. It was obvious that I was the black boy at the back of the bus. Maybe he thought I was hiding weed or had a concealed weapon. I call this being guilty until proven innocent. All he found was a bus pass, my house keys and my badge for work.

It wasn't just officers of the law who treated with me this lack of respect. During my final years at school, I chose to take design technology as an option. It was a big mistake – my teacher for the subject was determined to make my life hell for a few hours a week, every week. One incident I can still remember vividly today starts off with me at home the night before completing my homework. I'd run out of the standard A3 size paper that we normally used and had to use A4. The next day when my teacher Mr. Davies was collecting everyone's homework. I noticed quite a few students hadn't used the

A3 size paper but once he got to me, he asked "What's that? Go and sit over there." He pointed to the other students who hadn't submitted any homework and wouldn't be participating in practical work that day. I didn't hold my tongue, "What do you mean, what's that?" I asked. "It's homework; you can't stop me from doing practical today. I've seen you not have a problem with at least four other people." I didn't ask what was different about me; he'd made that clear months ago. Instead, I chose to call him out for the first time. "You're a racist, you are a racist" with a cheeky smirk he said, "you're a racist" mimicking and making fun of me. "I'll let you off this time, but don't do it again." He was happy to use his position to threaten students but was too much of a coward to follow through. Imagine if all of my teachers treated me like this. I wouldn't have finished school and achieved the level of education I have today, which consists of GCSE's (finishing school), multiple A-Levels, and a law degree. Yet even after all of this, I still considered myself one of the "lucky ones."

So, what does this all mean? What is the world teaching us through modern history? I'm getting to that point where I think enough is enough. We as minorities and people of color have an important choice to make. History has repeated itself time and time again. There have been countless marches and movements, but all seem to end in death. So, the way I see it, is either there is an inevitable civil war brewing and ready to explode or a mass exodus in which we return to our homelands, drop the anchor, and build up those communities, leaving these false dreams behind. Our ancestors came here seeking a better life and that was heavily due to the fact that they were influenced by colonizers. Yet three, going on four, generations later, that "better life" hasn't worked out. Only a small percentage of people of color have "made it" and "live the dream." The rest are left to suffer and struggle. So will another war change that or cause more bloodshed and maybe lower a few voices until the courage to fight hate and injustice returns.

At least in our regions of origin, our success and achievement will be solely based on merit, because looking around we will all look similar, not the same, and face no double standards. I've definitely made up my mind on retirement, once I'm over 40 getting close to 50 and have gained more power and control over my life, I'll be looking to make a move back to the Caribbean unless dramatic change occurs that creates a fair and inclusive future for all.

The most recent global marches that were sparked after the unlawful killing of George Floyd, an unarmed American Black man. An on-duty police officer knelt on his neck for 8 minutes and 46 seconds until Floyd was no longer breathing. I do want to say this – rest in power George Floyd. I hope your death will not be in vain. The response to this injustice has been groundbreaking and, in all honesty, different than anything I've seen in my lifetime. Turning on the news and watching the marches, I see people of all backgrounds coming together to fight for a brighter future for all, so maybe this time it really will be different. I have chosen to not join the marches as I already knew thousands would, I have chosen to use my platform and position in my career to fight for change and help shape the path for the next generation as minorities are hit the hardest inside the hearts and minds of children. Dreams and ambitions are crushed when there are no equal opportunities and or role models to look up to. I'm determined to build a future where if you're a young black boy or girl you don't need to feel like you can only be successful as an athlete, musician, or actor. I'm pushing to create a world where the right role models are held up and highlighted in all professions to show the younger generation that they can do it and here is the golden ticket to get you there, that golden ticket being the beaten path of those who came before you. Say for example you had a passion for science and medicine, a lot of people won't be aware of Mary Seacole, a great heroic figure in black history from Kingston Jamaica who doesn't get half the recognition of someone like Florence Nightingale which really makes no sense to me.

The Film Hidden Figures showed that we would have never made it into space as soon as we did without the mathematical minds of Katherine Johnson, Dorothy Vaughan, and Mary Jackson, three black women who were part of NASA's team of human "computers." They calculated the equations that sent the likes of Neil Armstrong into space. Think about what a movie like that can do for that young black girl who loves mathematics. I can't believe I was 26 before I learned about these pioneering women. It is critical that Black historical figures are not overlooked in classroom history lessons. They are exceptional role models who should be highlighted and celebrated just as much as their Caucasian counterparts. That's a change I'm still waiting to see. Until then, I'll continue to choose to colour outside the lines of the curriculum to seek the broader truths.

During my three years as a law student, I learned the differences between right and wrong. It might actually be more accurate to say I learned the differences between fair and the law. Early on, I was stunned by the fact that laws can be interpreted by the adjudicators, whether that be a judge or lay magistrate, in a number of ways. These are the Literal, Golden, and Mischief rules.

The Literal rule means a judge should primarily be concerned with the literal words of the legislation. The Golden rule allows a judge to depart from a statute's normal meaning to avoid a ridiculous result. The Mischief rule is applied to recognise what "mischief" Parliament was attempting to rectify.

Here's a real-life scenario. I was on my way home from University and got stopped on a train by a ticket inspector who asked to see my train ticket. I showed him my student travel card for the month, he then asked for my Student Railcard I.D. For whatever reason, I didn't have it on me that day, which gave the inspector the leverage he was looking for to issue me a penalty fine. I argued my point; but he wouldn't listen. It's clear here that the law was put in place to stop people from abusing the discount system and to ensure everyone pays the correct fare, not to catch students who might have rushed out one morning without grabbing every form of I.D. they might need that day. Either way, the inspector chose to abuse his power and issue me with a fine, which I later appealed. On the surface, it looks like I broke the law and was traveling without a valid ticket because for a student ticket to be valid, you must be a student. Inspectors can usually confirm this by seeing your Student Railcard I.D. Another way they can confirm this is by using the same radio they use to double check addresses to ensure your name is in the student database. Regardless, I wasn't going to let that ruin my day. Instead, I chose to use it as an opportunity to practice the skills I'd been learning at law school, take the ticket and craft a response to clearly explain my innocence in the form of an appeal. Education is important because knowledge is power, and power is everything.

Having knowledge and knowing how to use it played a huge role in my growth during my 20s. I'm sure it will continue to help me for the rest of my life. Pursuing personal development over traditional education is what began to set me apart from most of the people I grew up around. Raising the bar for yourself and becoming the best version of you is easily the best choice you'll ever make in life.

4 CAREER AND OWNING YOUR DESTINY

My first experience in the corporate world occurred during an "assessment day" put on by a recruitment firm called Celsius. "Celsius" was a play on words as they only recruited soon to be graduates with degrees – get it? Anyway, Celsius approached me at a career fair my university put on towards the end of the semester. All students were encouraged to at least attend and look around. At the time, I had my sights set on a career in law but didn't have plans that weekend and went to the fair with an open mind. I didn't stay too long and maybe did one lap around the room. I spoke to a few people and headed for the exit. But just as I was about to leave, a guy grabbed me, complimented me on my appearance and pitched me on this idea of an assessment day, competing against a group of students from various universities. The only word I needed to hear was "competition." I love to compete, so I couldn't resist. "Sign me up, I'll be there."

At the assessment day, a group of about 10 soon to be graduates arrived. I was the only Black guy, but I kind of expected that since it was held slightly outside of London in St Albans. We were told we'd compete in a series of challenges and by the end of the day, only a few of us would be left. Think of the TV show The Apprentice but condensed down into one day (and without the cameras).

The first challenge was simple: one by one, stand up, tell us who you are, what you're studying, where you're from, who inspires you and why. After about the fifth person, I was getting bored with the cookie-cutter answers: Warren Buffet and Bill Gates. It was like every student had prepared the same speech. Finally, it was my turn and I already knew who I was going to say. I always stayed true to myself and never let peer pressure get the best of me. "Hi, I'm Frank, I was born in the Bahamas, I'm studying law and my biggest inspiration is Curtis 50 Cent Jackson." The whole room burst into laughter – they thought it was a joke. So I waited for giggles to stop and repeated myself. "I'm serious, 50 Cent is my inspiration, you all probably know him as a rapper. But did you know he made millions out of his first record deal? The thing I like about Fifty is he doesn't know when to stop, isn't afraid of competition, and finds success anywhere he goes. Has anyone seen his movies? He has a clothing line too. But he didn't stop there, he's selling flavored bottled water called formula50 and even though he works with Dr. Dre who currently sells "Beats" headphones, he still sells his own line, called SMS Audio. Fifty inspires me because if you give him a challenge, he'll find a way to overcome it. He never gives up." I didn't add this next part, but just between you and I, the other reason he inspires me is that he's also a black man who grew up in a less affluent area which meant seeing him accomplish all those goals showed me that I could do the same.

The room was stunned, shocked, and didn't know how to act. You could hear a pin drop. Picture a small room with mostly white males in suits, a few women and me. Everyone was sitting down, and I was standing in the middle of the room giving this speech. Faced with a moment that for everyone else made them feel bigger or better than me, it quickly turned out to be a moment for me to captivate the audience and show them it's okay to be yourself and walk your own path. This choice to display independence and fearlessness played a huge role in gaining the attention of those who we'll call "watchers" for the time being. The day was filled with other group and solo challenges including mock cold calls, verbal reasoning concepts, and ultimately ended with the final three of us going through to mock interviews. I was asked to wait behind at the end of the day – a woman, "one of the watchers" wanted to speak with me. This lady turned out to be a hiring manager for the company that would later become my first employer. This company offered me a job before I had even graduated.

FEAR

The first time I lost, I lost big and it almost broke me. I was working as a letting agent in South London, renting apartments for a respectable brand. I took this role at the recommendation of a good friend. Before this, I was working for a small I.T. software company, from the assessment day, and doing a two-hour commute (one way). It wasn't sustainable. My friend reached out with a solution to my problem – a job near home with a young, outgoing team. We even got to drive company cars. At the time, it felt like a no brainer.

Looking back now, it probably wasn't the best career choice, though it did strengthen our friendship, which was the biggest takeaway for me. Here's what happened. In less than a year, I knew I didn't love what I was doing, and I had known this for some time. It had begun to affect my work, but I ignored it because success always seemed to come easy to me. I never really had to work that hard to achieve and be successful. I guess you can say this was a wake-up call.

Then something crazy happened. I crashed, both figuratively and physically. My performance numbers dropped, and I totaled the BMW 1 series the company provided to me. I resigned the next day, thinking that I would pick up a new role in the blink of an eye. I figured that as long as I put my resume out there, I would be employed again real soon. It was a big mistake. A few months passed and I hadn't secured a new role. My money and little savings were gone and almost immediately, I lost the feeling of independence. It was crushing. At the time I can remember getting ready to fall asleep one night just to get past the anxiety.

Bouncing back, I woke up the next day determined to win and vowing to never allow myself to feel that way ever again. I put pressure on myself to step up my game. I spent the next three days on my laptop looking for and applying for sales roles, writing cover letters and pitching myself to recruitment agents so they would prioritise my search over others. I had one song on repeat, "Rags to Riches" by Lisa "Left Eye" Lopes featuring Andre Rison. Side note: Apple Music needs to add this song to its digital catalog – its energy is infectious. Within a few weeks, I had control again, I was presented with three roles: one with a property investment firm based in Dubai, one with Softcat, one of the largest I.T. resellers in Europe, and one with a local business search and review site, Yelp. The last of the three doesn't sound too sexy on the face of it, but that interview process ignited a fire in me. The employees were diverse, the sales team was huge and included people from all walks of life. I instantly felt at home and will forever appreciate my time at Yelp.

I'm sure you've heard the saying, "don't drink too much of the Kool-Aid; you don't know what's in it." After a year and a half of working for Yelp, this saying came up time and time again. I understood what it meant – don't blindly follow something without doing your own due diligence. There's a darker origin to the phrase but I'll let you look that one up in your own time. Still, at the time, I guess I wasn't aware that my role as an account executive at the bottom of the organisation meant that I was just another number in the system and that I could be replaced at any time.

My value didn't represent my worth. I learned that lesson the hard way when Yelp pulled out of Europe and other international locations to retreat to the U.S. They left us with fair severance packages but for me, I was back at square one. I needed to find a job.

DISAPPOINTMENT

The second time I lost, I should've known better and seen it coming. I did a short stint a very very early stage startup who had way too many emerging challenges which it made it hard for me to see how and when it would ever become profitable, So I decided to cut my losses and joined Trustpilot after being referred by the same friend who brought me into the lettings market all those years ago.

This time, it felt like a better fit for me. it was SaaS, this stands for software as a service, and it was reminiscent of the value proposition we lived and breathed by back at Yelp, this being the power of word of mouth. But what I hadn't yet firmly grasped is that when it comes to choosing a career path, you end up working for companies that produce one of two things: must-have products and services and nice-to-have products and services. As much as I enjoyed my time at Yelp, much like Trustpilot, it offered a nice-to-have service.

Choosing to spend your time building a career with a company that creates nice-to-have products is dangerous. Believe me, I've done it twice. You can either take my word for it or find out the hard way that's your choice.

So what went wrong. You could call it a combination of arrogance and impatience, but 18 months into my time at Trustpilot I chose to head for door without having anything lined up, thinking by now I know what it takes to find work and had planned to use my savings to give myself time to write a business plan.

I had done some research and found the perfect resource to get this done, a book from the Financial Times called Writing a Business Plan: How to Win Backing to Start Up or Grow Your Business. It was exactly what I needed. Fast forwarded three months. The business plan was complete, and I had an investor lined up to support me in launching a fitness app. I pulled the plug at the last minute as at the time I didn't believe I was ready to run my own business.

I felt like I needed more exposure in successful companies to fill in my knowledge gaps. However, this was the least of my problems as the start of the month was coming up with all bills including rent being due. I was running out of money and by now I had moved out on my own. Let's just say my mum was my saving grace and covered me, a luxury I know we all don't have.

Getting past the slump, I picked myself up and looked again at the employment market armed with everything I learned from my past mistakes. I knew I had to find something better than everything I'd done before. I knew I needed to work with a product or service that was considered a "must-have." And I knew I wasn't going to settle for being just a number in the system again. Enter Duo Security.

PREPARATION

To prevent a third loss, I looked to this quote from Michael Jordan, the greatest basketball player and possibly the greatest athlete ever. "I've failed over and over and over again in my life. And that is why I succeed." I was looking to do exactly that, minus the third "over." If I can

Taking the humble approach and utilising my professional network, I secured a role at Duo Security relatively quickly, coming in on the ground floor as an ADR who just books meetings. After already having six years of sales experience in a variety of industries, I had to make a choice to not be egocentric and get my ego out of the way, and I'm glad I did.

Coming in, I had very little knowledge of cybersecurity and what drove the industry. So, I viewed my first year at Duo like a student would his freshman year at University. But with such open and honest prospects and customers alike, my first 12 months didn't feel like a baptism of fire. Thank God, lol. What I did learn was a wealth of knowledge coming straight from the horse's mouth. I quickly began to understand what Duo's mission of democratizing security truly meant and why Duo's customers loved it so much.

I was going from strength to strength, collecting two MVP awards back to back in consecutive years. They called me the "Meet Machine" because I was relentlessly booking meetings. At the time, our inbound leads model was a key part of growing the business; every meeting counted. It was like I was meant to be there, and I walked in at the right moment. To top it all off, I built relationships with people within the business who truly cared about my professional development. They taught me the importance of personal brand, emotional intelligence, humility and how to defensively differentiate myself from the competition.

I've watched Duo scale to unicorn status and court a $2.35 billion-dollar acquisition from Cisco, the largest networking company in the world. This acquisition changed a few things. On the positive side, it gave us as a sales team the ability to connect with thousands of new customers and prospects by leveraging existing Cisco relationships. On the negative side, we saw slower progress on product development and turnover of staff. Not everyone wants to work for a huge company; they prefer startups and smaller firms.

My main takeaway from this experience has been this: become

invaluable and as close to irreplaceable as possible. Three and half years later, I'm still at Duo Security, now part of Cisco. It's been, and continues to be, an unforgettable experience. I've managed to elevate my position to Head of Inside Sales for all of Europe, the Middle East, South Africa and Russia.

There have been a few keys to my success.

Firstly, I've stayed hungry for knowledge. When successful businesses grow and personnel turnover, those who remain and have a wealth of knowledge and understanding of the business grow in value. So, go out of your way to absorb as much information as physically possible.

Secondly, I've built my team and network. We've had some of the most epic company days and nights out, trips abroad you name it, we love to get everyone together, but be deliberate with how you choose to use these limited pockets of time. A great quote from Deepak Chopra's book, Negotiating the Impossible, is "if you're not at the table, you're on the menu." I believe this to mean, if there are decisions being made at a higher level that impacts you specifically, career-wise, and you're not involved in those conversations then make sure there are people who have your back involved in those conversations, so your best interests are taking into consideration. This is easier said than done, but to put it simply, build honest and transparent relationships with "those who sit above in shadow."

These are the people who can look out for you and support the motions that move you forward. Take advantage of every opportunity to demonstrate your worth because you never know who's watching, listening, and planning for the future.

Finally, never, ever, take your foot off the gas as a young professional. There's no time or reason for me to be slowing down anytime soon. Let's open this up a bit and explore the importance of speed here. Every sales leader I meet tells me: "run faster," "fail quickly and early" and "time kills deals." Time is one of these god-like factors we just cannot control. Time costs nothing to spend, but if time is wasted that'll cost you in progress, so there are two ways to approach this.

The first way is to simply find more time, outwork both your peers and competition, take fewer breaks, start earlier and finish later. This deliberate sacrifice immediately gives you an edge.

In Dan Pink's book When, he shares the idea of three different birds: owls, which get up late and stay up late, larks who get up early and go to bed early, and the "third birds" who are somewhere in the middle. Figure out which type of bird you are and adjust your day accordingly.

To take this one step further, prioritise your workload so that you can tackle your most important work when you're at your best. Everyone's day consists of a peak, valley and a rebound. The peak is when you're at your best and the rebound isn't too far off. When you're in the valleys, you'll want to spend time on the least important tasks.

The second way to address the issue of time is to work smarter. This will require more skills and attention to detail, but it's absolutely achievable. At a high level, identify what works best and zero in on those "bright spots" to understand what's influencing these desired outcomes and do more of it, to contrast also identify what's not working and do less, if any, of that. Albert Einstein defined insanity as "doing the same thing over and over again and expecting a different result." Unless you're clinically insane, we don't need to challenge Einstein's IQ here.

To take this one step further, use the 80/20 rule for efficiency. This is also known as the "Pareto Principle." It advises that you spend 20% of your time planning what to do and 80% of your time executing your plan. Procrastination is the enemy.

Lastly, remember that **IRON SHARPENS IRON**. I can't stress how important it is to have true friends who are following the same, or a similar, path as your own. The friend I mentioned earlier in this chapter shares a lot of the same dreams as me. He knew this even before I did and valued our friendship more and more as time went on. He's shown and continues to show empathy each time I'm faced with a challenge inside and outside of the workplace. I know as we continue to progress in our careers and move towards our goals, we'll have each other's backs and lift one another up. I value this friendship highly and it has influenced me to be selective in the company   I   keep.

5 PERSONAL FINANCE, CHANGING THE GAME

When I was 19, I made a bet with my older cousin over who would make a million first. I'll never forget "Summertime 09." It had a ring to it and was filled with countless memories. It felt like we went to endless parties, always had time to be creative and spent way more money than we should have. (God knows I wasn't saving a penny back then). I'm 30 now and things are different. I'm still on this journey to make my first million, having made substantial progress over the past decade. But it's time to double down even further.

Many wise people have advised to surround yourself with the right people, or people on the same mission as you. With that same intent, I plan to surround myself with as many millionaires as I can, then figure out what they have in common (other than the obvious) and understand what they have done and/or are doing that I'm not. I need to expose my blind spots and lean in on this element of self-awareness. If I'm being honest, no one is going to hand me a million pounds. It's entirely down to me to make this happen and by making the right choices, I'm confident I'll get there.

Test the waters. I have always been interested in the stock market. But I never acted on my curiosity until I turned 28 – I guess I didn't want to get burned. I began to dabble in stocks, opening up a few brokerage accounts on platforms like eToro, Hargreaves Lansdown, and most recently Freetrade. I tested them all and found Freetrade to be the most user friendly. This is now my go-to for investing in the stock market. I choose stocks that make sense to me and try not to overcomplicate things. My first principle is "belief in the brand." If I don't use a brand's products or services regularly, I don't believe in the brand.

From there, I listen to intuition. Any resistance to this principle requires extensive research and we have already covered the importance of time in the last chapter. I want to make this process as easy as possible for me.

To begin with, I build a laundry list of brands I believe in, then to boil this list down by seeking credible advice on performance forecasts and other factors that impact share prices. To date, I've found the "Robinhood Snacks" podcast to be insightful, entertaining and digestible. The podcast is published daily during the week and is only about 15 to 20 minutes long. I'll then cross-reference this with the company's quarterly earnings. Right before I pull the trigger, I check the share price's year on year growth – it's 52-week low and 52-week high. After all that, I make a call if I consider it a good time to get in and if I can see a positive trend, which means its price is moving up and to the right. It's that simple.

Now we all know Warren Buffet said, "time in the market beats timing the market." That's certainly true, but I've found that using the steps outlined above provides opportunities to get in and out. And most importantly, it provides opportunities to profit.

Diversification. Never put all of your money in one place. You'll want to spread the risk. This is probably the first piece of financial advice that caught my attention. Learning about alternative assets and alternative investment options fascinates me. But before I rush into anything too onerous, I'll seek professional financial advice. I know I'm definitely not the first person who wants to see my money work for itself and make more money. That means that I'll always consult the geniuses and experts of the past and present for advice when necessary.

Setting a high bar. Seneca the Younger, a Roman philosopher, said "luck is what happens when preparation meets opportunity." This couldn't be truer in my life. my most recent career transitions being the most vivid example. As a sales rep, I always strived to be the best on the team, not because I wanted to gloat and show off, but because I wanted to sharpen my skills in every aspect of the role so that I could never be overlooked. What I didn't know at the time was that my then team manager had been making plans to move on, leaving an open vacancy that needed to be filled.

I hesitated at first, but after seeking advice from my inner circle and receiving an overwhelming level of encouragement, I put myself forward, not actually expecting to get the role. But who's the better appointee – a manager from another division within our parent company or outside talent who would need at least six months to get up to speed on product knowledge and our internal process? We were already halfway through the financial year, so I was almost an unbeatable choice. But I was only able to capitalise on this because I had worked hard to put myself in a position to not be overlooked. I was actually working towards another senior role which was vacant, and I had an agreed career path to get there, which meant there were already a lot of eyes on me.

When you set goals that are sky high and work intelligently towards them, something magical happens – you tend to achieve those goals. The SMART goals structure of ensuring your goals are specific, measurable, attainable, realistic and time-measured can be adopted in any aspect of your life.

Take the bet I made with my cousin over who would make a million first. We specified it to be a million, it's measurable by definition, achievable in my eyes because there are approximately 46.8 million millionaires in the world, that's a lot of blueprints or golden tickets to follow, and that makes it realistic, the only mistake we made was leaving out "time." So, I've decided right now to put a five-year time limit on it. I honestly believe it gives me enough time.

Breaking this down, this means I need to gain $200,000 every year for the next five years. 2018 data from the Seattle Times showed that 56% of American households earned $200,000, and the HMRC states that in the UK, the top 10% of the nation earned an annual income of £176,000 ($217,000). A quick Google search of "how to make $200,000 per year" returns results with a list of careers – sales being at the top (which is convenient for me). But Remember, I am not choosing to rely on one revenue stream to get there; there's too much risk in that.

THE AVERAGE MILLIONAIRE HAS SEVEN SOURCES OF INCOME.

One, earned income – that's the day job.

Two – profit Income, that means buying something then later selling it for a profit. I stick to blue-chip shares on the stock market which hasn't failed me yet.

Three – interest income. To check this box, I hold multiple ISAs which provide the best interest rates banks have to offer with tax benefits.

Four – dividend income. I'm good there – a handful of my blue-chip stocks pay me dividends quarterly.

Five – rental income. I don't currently own a rental property but have been toying with the idea of purchasing a car in full and having it rented out through one of the many car rental platforms like "Drivy" or "Turo." But I should mention a rental property isn't out of the question.

Six – capital gains. This is the profit gained by selling an asset for more than you purchased it. It's similar to profit. If I combine the gain in my brokerage accounts and my employee stock purchase plan, I've got this well underway.

Finally, seven – royalty income. If I'm successful in publishing this book and it gains traction among readers, I'll be due some healthy royalties.

You can quickly start to see that my goal setting isn't outrageous and is actually entirely achievable. It just requires focus, drive, discipline and determination – strengths I've already highlighted. Now, I need to use them to my advantage.

Something I wish someone would have told me at 21 is to "overthink payday." It sounds dramatic, but I'm serious; plan for it so when it comes, you can execute with optimum efficiency. I approach my monthly paycheck in the same way each month. First, I take out my essential outgoings such as bills, budget for travel and food. Then from there, I deduct a large percentage for investing and savings. What's left is disposable income, which I can use for social events, quality time with my partner, family and friends and then some retail therapy depending on my mood.

With this approach, I'm always increasing my future net worth and spending power first, rather than blowing the budget on £1000 trainers, club tables, and other useless objects I see so many hyping up on Instagram. My mum always taught me to keep a rainy-day fund. Lord knows when it rains, it pours. You're going to need a little nest egg to get you through the dark days.

Personal Banking. Up until recently, I was unaware that the major UK banks limit our choices in personal baking using a class system based on income, level of spending power, savings and assets held.

Let's say for example that your annual income surpasses £100,000. All of sudden, you're considered a desirable customer and with this, your bank will be willing to shower you in perks and resources such as 24/7 concierge services to handle booking shows, holidays and events, grant you unlimited access to hundreds of airport lounges across the world, one on one support for a complex financial decision, home and travel insurance and more. It almost sounds as if the more you earn, the "easier" life becomes.

But remember, although the products we purchase and the experiences we pay for bring us joy, money itself can't buy you happiness.   That   always   comes   from   within.

6 CLOSING THOUGHTS

Life isn't easy. But it wouldn't be much fun if it were. We're all going to be faced with challenging times and dishonest or dishonorable people. It's how we choose to look at and learn from these moments that make all the difference.

You're the hero of your own movie; choose to color outside the lines. The greatest choices you'll ever make are those that support you being yourself, betting on yourself and putting your best foot forward. You'll have to play to your strengths, and work on your weaknesses by learning from those who came before you and keeping close company with those who believe in you, and only want you to experience the best.

Choose today because tomorrow never comes. That's why it's tomorrow. And if you're aiming high enough, I'll be honest with you, you'll need to bring you A game every day. And no matter how bad it gets, keep your chin up and stick to the plan. You got this.

Choices

Frank Chevannes

Printed in Great Britain
by Amazon

51527238R00037